The BreakThrough Series

SECRETS
of
THE VINE

Breaking Through to Abundance

BRUCE
WILKINSON

WITH DAVID KOPP

Multnomah Books

SECRETS OF THE VINE
published by Multnomah Books
A division of Random House, Inc.

© 2001 by Ovation Foundation, Inc.
International Standard Book Number: 978-1-59052-496-1

Scripture quotations are from:
The Holy Bible, New King James Version
© 1984 by Thomas Nelson, Inc.

The Holy Bible, New International Version (NIV)
© 1973, 1984 by International Bible Society,
used by permission of Zondervan Publishing House

Holy Bible, New Living Translation (NLT)
© 1996. Used by permission of Tyndale House Publishers, Inc.
All rights reserved.

Secrets of the Vine® is a registered trademark of Multnomah Books.

Multnomah and its mountain colophon are registered trademarks
of Random House, Inc.
Printed in the United States of America
ALL RIGHTS RESERVED

For information:
MULTNOMAH BOOKS
12265 ORACLE BOULEVARD, SUITE 200
COLORADO SPRINGS, CO 80921

2008
16

TABLE OF CONTENTS

For disciples who have ever wondered if a life of extraordinary abundance just might be their birthright.

To my friend and writing partner David Kopp, and to our assisting editor, Heather Harpham Kopp—sincere thanks for the skill and caring you have brought to this book. Working with both of you is a joy.

To Don Jacobson and the entire Multnomah publishing team—I am so thankful to know you and work with you. May you rejoice as the fruit of your ministry reaches around the world for Christ.

PREFACE

Dear Reader,

Abundance—that beautiful overflow of true worth in a person's life—is exactly what you and I were born for. No wonder we so deeply desire it! Yet millions of Christians settle for less because they misunderstand and resist God's ways of bringing it about.

In *The Prayer of Jabez*, I showed readers how to ask for a life of abundant impact and significance for God. In *Secrets of the Vine*, I want to show you how God works in your life to answer that prayer—and what you can do to cooperate with Him to make it happen. You'll be surprised to discover how much God *wants* abundance for you. And you'll be relieved to know that you never need to misread His ways in your life again.

That's why I invite you to read this little book with an open heart and great hope.

Sincerely,
Bruce Wilkinson

STORIES FROM THE VINEYARD

*H*ave you ever been with someone very close to you who is about to die, someone who loves you and wants to leave you with a final word? "Come closer." You lean close, straining to hear.

"I want to tell you something. I've waited until now...but I can't wait any longer."

You know that you'll remember every word for the rest of your life.

Now imagine that the person who is about to speak is Jesus. How closely would you listen? How long and hard would you ponder your Lord's last words to you?

In the pages to come, I invite you to encounter, perhaps for the first time, Jesus' words in John 15—the heart of His final message to His disciples on the night He was betrayed. By dusk the following day, Jesus would be stretched out on a cross, His body stripped and pierced, His life ebbing away.

Jesus knew the words He spoke that night would echo in His friends' memories for years. In time, the truth of His "deathbed conversation" would lead them to a whole new way of thinking. These final words are so little understood today that I've called them "secrets," but I'm convinced that Jesus meant for their meaning to be clear. The time for parables and hidden meanings had passed. He wanted every follower for generations to come to know exactly how to live an overflowing life and understand what God would do to make it happen.

These final words are so little understood today that I've called them "secrets."

Watch how the Savior carefully and tenderly chooses the moment to speak.

THURSDAY NIGHT UPSTAIRS

If you've been a Christian for a while, you've probably heard a lot about the upper room—the scene of the climactic evening meal Jesus had with His disciples. You can easily imagine, then, the men around the table reclining on pillows, their faces turned toward the Master. You can hear the muted conversation. You can smell the aroma of freshly baked bread and of roasted lamb and onions.

It is the night before Passover, the Jewish day to remember the nation's escape from slavery in Egypt. Hundreds of thousands have come to Jerusalem to celebrate, and this year more than ever the city is buzzing with rumors about Messiah. More than one prophet has predicted that on just such a day, Messiah will arrive to deliver Israel from all of her oppressors forever.

But these men reclining around the table know something the crowds outside don't. Messiah is already here. He is with them here in the room.

The disciples have spent three years with Him, and one by one they've come to the same conclusion: Jesus of Nazareth *is* Messiah—the One worth risking everything to follow. In fact, the disciples are so certain about how the events of Passover week will unfold that they have spent a good part of the journey from Galilee arguing about who will get which position of honor in the new kingdom.

Dinner begins.

Peter, pass the lamb.

Hey James, let's get to the temple early. I don't want to miss ten thousand angels teaching those Roman legions a lesson.

Psst, Matthew! I'd say our money woes are about to be history!

The disciples expect that these lamplit hours among friends in the upper room will carry on into the evening, poignant but peaceful, full of toasts to the good years to come. But things begin to unravel.

THE UNRAVELING

The apostle John recorded the exact moment the mood changed:

> *And supper being ended. . . Jesus. . . rose from supper and laid aside His garments, took a towel and girded Himself. After that, He poured water into a basin and began to wash the disciples' feet, and to wipe them with the towel with which He was girded.* (John 13:2–5)

Shocked, the men can only watch in shame as Messiah swabs grime from between their toes. Water plinks into the bowl. The disciples shift nervously, not daring to speak. Why would tomorrow's king behave like tonight's houseboy?

It gets worse. "Most assuredly, I say to you, one of you will betray Me," Jesus announces (v. 21). The stunned men look around the circle. Then comes the clincher. Jesus tells Peter that before sunup, he will deny his Lord three times. An awful realization begins to dawn: Their whole mission is doomed.

Of course, Jesus has been trying to tell them for months that His appointment in Jerusalem is with a cross, not a throne. But His warnings have been mixed with predictions that Messiah is about to return in power and glory, and the disciples have heard what they wanted to hear.

But tonight Jesus strips away their last hopes. "A little while longer and the world will see Me no more," He says, "but you will see Me." That rules out any public triumph.

Jesus presses on. The final blow sounds like a concession statement: "I will no longer talk much with you, for the ruler of this world is coming." That can mean only one thing: Jesus is *not* the ruler; He will *not* be King.

Now I see pain written all over the disciples' faces. Listen with me to Jesus' words. Out of context they seem serene, almost hopeful. But in the crisis of this room, each phrase mirrors the emotional devastation of His men. Listen to His words...then watch their faces:

Little children... They're feeling small and weak.

I have loved you... They're staring at Him in disbelief, mistrust, and fear.

Let not your heart be troubled... They're sinking in anxiety and dread.

I will not leave you orphans... They're slumping before Him like abandoned children, defenseless in a hostile world.

> *They're staring at Him in disbelief, mistrust, and fear.*

The evening in the upper room ends. The questions end. Into the silence, Jesus says, "Arise, let us go from here" (John 14:31).

LIGHT IN THE VINEYARD

Eleven dejected men follow Jesus down the stairs and out into the cool night air. Some of the disciples carry lamps or burning torches to light the way. Perhaps Jesus tells them where He is heading—to a garden on the Mount of Olives where they often spent time. Perhaps they already know. But I believe that as their footsteps echo through the narrow streets, not a word is spoken.

The disciples follow Jesus down the hill, through the

winding streets of Jerusalem. Avoiding the temple mount and its noisy, celebrating crowds, Jesus turns right and leads them out of the city. Then they turn sharply left to follow the Kidron Valley up toward their destination.

Along the terraces that follow the curve of the valley, they pass through ancient vineyards. They walk in single file between rows of neatly tended grapes, plants that have been bearing fruit for generations. To the left above them tower the city walls and the ramparts of the temple. Ahead and to the right rises the Mount of Olives, where Gethsemane and betrayal await.

Here Jesus stops. Hemmed in by rows of vines, the disciples gather around. Lamps and torches sputter in the night air and flicker in their eyes.

Jesus reaches for a grape branch. Showing signs of new spring growth, its woody stem lies across His hand in the golden light. Now He begins. "I am the true vine, and My Father is the vinedresser" (15:1).

In the next few minutes Jesus talks quietly about branches and grapes and how a vinedresser cares for his prize vineyard. It certainly isn't what His disciples expect to hear. But this is the moment Jesus chooses to reveal their surprising destiny.

THE CURTAINS OF HEAVEN

Too many Christians I've met are standing in the shadows of that vineyard. Like the disciples, they have discovered that following Jesus has turned out far differently than expected. They feel confused and disillusioned—maybe even betrayed by God.

Do you? If so, listen carefully—I believe that a major reason for your spiritual crisis may be that you have not heard and understood Jesus' words in the vineyard.

Lamps and torches sputter in the night air and flicker in their eyes.

For decades of my life as a Christian, I didn't understand, either. And because I didn't, I fell out of fellowship. I struggled against God. I settled for a spiritual experience often characterized by disappointment, doubt, and even anger. Looking back, I see that I was still thinking about a God who would help me win on my own terms. I had failed to lean close and listen.

But over the years, I was drawn back again and again into that lamplit circle, and what I finally heard there has brought freedom and joy into my life. Now I understand what God wants from me—a fruitful harvest for Him. And now I can see how He has been at work all along in my life to bring that about.

Will you take to heart what Jesus said in those crucial, final moments? Every word matters. Jesus wants to pull back the curtains of heaven for you just as He did for His disciples.

You see, Jesus was thinking of you, too, that night. I'm sure of it. In cautious Thomas and reckless Peter, in guileless Nathaniel and scheming James, He saw and loved you, too. And I believe He has lovingly directed you to this little book just as purposefully as He led His closest friends into that vineyard.

The secrets of the vine that I will show you in the chapters to come are our Father's amazing plan to keep His children flourishing—physically, emotionally, and spiritually. In fact, we could call them family secrets because they're really only meaningful to disciples like you who have followed your Lord all the way here...past the celebration, outside the city walls, straight into the dark.

2

WHAT GOD
WANTS

*T*hink of some things Jesus did *not* put in His hand to make His point that night in the vineyard.

Not money.

Not a map for a military (or angelic) invasion of Jerusalem.

Not a letter explaining to all the wives back home just what the last three years were supposed to have been about.

Jesus was thinking of grapes. Holding the branch of a mature grapevine, He said:

> *"I am the true vine, and My Father is the vinedresser. Every branch in Me that does not bear fruit He takes away; and every branch that bears fruit He prunes, that it may bear*

more fruit. I am the vine, you are the branches. He who abides in Me, and I in him, bears much fruit. By this My Father is glorified, that you bear much fruit." (John 15:1–2, 5, 8)

Are pictures coming to your mind? Can you feel the ragged bark, the curl of a tendril, the fuzzy surface of new leaves? Can you smell the spicy sweetness of the grapes?

Jesus loved to convey the deepest truths with simple, earthy examples. In His last message before His death, He wanted you and me to comprehend with our whole being that He has left us on this planet for one compelling reason—and it has everything to do with fruit.

Jesus loved to convey the deepest truths with simple, earthy examples.

An Old Vineyard, A New Perspective

Inside the metaphor of the vineyard, Jesus introduced a picture to help us understand our role in bearing fruit for God.

1. Jesus is the vine. If you didn't grow up in wine country, you might think that the vine is a long, trailing limb that sprawls along the trellis. Actually, it's the trunk of the plant that grows out of the ground. Vineyard keepers traditionally keep the vine at waist height—thirty-six to forty-two inches. The vine ends in a large gnarl from which branches grow in either direction along the trellis.

2. *The Father is the vinedresser.* The vinedresser is the keeper of the vineyard—either the owner or the person hired to tend it. The vinedresser's task is simple—to coax from his plants the most pounds of grapes possible. A healthy and properly tended vineyard means a higher yield.

3. *You and I are branches.* In the vineyard, the branches are the focus of the vinedresser's efforts because they produce the fruit. Branches are tied to a trellis or propped up with sticks to let air circulate, to provide the maximum amount of sunshine, and to allow full access for tending. The vinedresser lovingly cultivates each branch so that it will bear as much fruit as possible.

These images from the vineyard may be interesting from a horticultural point of view. But let me ask you: Why would Jesus talk in such detail about growing grapes when He was only hours from death and His best friends' hopes had just been crushed?

Clearly, Jesus knew that the time and place were right to show the disciples a new way of looking at things. Jesus wanted them to see their future from the perspective of heaven. He didn't want to leave them on earth wondering, *What is God up to in my life? And why isn't it turning out the way I expected?*

WHAT IS FRUIT?

For years I read this passage as a general call to Christians to bring others to Christ. But there's no reason to restrict Jesus' meaning of *fruit* to winning souls. I have traced the words *fruit* and *good works* in the Bible, and they're used nearly interchangeably. Take, for instance, this verse in Titus:

> *Let our people also learn to maintain good works, to meet urgent needs, that they may not be unfruitful.* (3:14)

The disciples wouldn't have interpreted Jesus' words to mean just evangelism, either. As people who lived close to nature, they would have understood that fruit symbolized the best result or sweetest prize in life.

They might have remembered these familiar words:

> *[The righteous man] shall be like a tree*
> *Planted by the rivers of water,*

That brings forth its fruit in its season,
  Whose leaf also shall not wither;
And whatever he does shall prosper. (Psalm 1:3)

In practical terms, fruit represents good works—a thought, attitude, or action of ours that God values because it glorifies Him. The fruit from your life is how God receives His due honor on earth. That's why Jesus declares, "By this My Father is glorified, that you bear much fruit" (John 15:8).

You bear inner fruit when you allow God to nurture in you a new, Christlike quality: "The fruit of the Spirit is love, joy, peace, longsuffering, kindness, goodness, faithfulness, gentleness, self-control" (Galatians 5:22).

You bear outward fruit when you allow God to work through you to bring Him glory. That would certainly include sharing your faith. The apostles saw every arena of life as an opportunity to bear fruit. Paul wrote, "God is able to make all grace abound to you, so

You'd think that something so crucial to God's plan would happen automatically.

that in all things at all times, having all that you need, you will abound in every good work" (2 Corinthians 9:8, NIV). Whether you're chopping wood for a widow, taking care of an ill neighbor, or spending a lifetime as a missionary in the jungle, outward fruit appears when your motive is to bring God glory.

How important and valuable is fruit bearing, then? Jesus says, "I chose you and appointed you that you should go and bear fruit, and that your fruit should remain" (John 15:16). Fruit is your only permanent deposit in heaven. Real fruit always lasts! And it's the main earthly reason you were saved. Paul told Christians they were "created in Christ Jesus for good works" (Ephesians 2:10).

Jesus hasn't led us to this torchlit circle just to make our dreams come true. Our dreams, like the disciples', are always too small. We are here to fulfill *God's* dream—that *we will bring Him glory through a remarkably abundant life.* That's how we find our greatest personal fulfillment, now and for eternity.

You'd think that something so crucial to God's plan would happen automatically in your life and mine. Nothing could be further from the truth. For the vineyard to really produce, the branches have to respond to the attentions of the vinedresser. But as we'll see, all branches do not respond alike. In fact, every branch in the vineyard is unique, and when harvest day arrives, each will have produced a different-sized crop.

Let's take our own walk in the vineyard. I'll show you four distinct levels of eternal yield. You're about to get a clear picture of what your life is adding up to for God at this very moment.

You guess that the vinedresser has already been here, probably at the crack of dawn.

BASKETS OF GLORY

It's an early morning during harvest season in vineyard country. You're out enjoying the fresh air when you find your path wending through a lovely hillside vineyard. Between each row you notice harvest baskets resting on the ground—one basket underneath each branch. You guess that the vinedresser has already been here, probably at the crack of dawn. You can tell by the way the baskets are placed that he's been testing his prospects. As you'd expect, the vinedresser wants to know before his harvest wagons rumble into town later in the week what kind of harvest he'll have to show for himself.

You pick up the first basket and look inside. You don't see any fruit. Not very encouraging—some branches don't bear a single grape. Jesus had this kind of branch in mind when He said, "Every branch in Me that *does not bear fruit*" (John 15:2).

You step over a row and peek into the second basket.

What a relief! You see several healthy clusters of grapes nestled in the bottom. Some branches, then, are not barren. You can find grapes on them if you look hard enough. Jesus described this branch as one that "bears *fruit*" (v. 2). Still, not much to get excited about here. You start to wonder about the skill of the vinedresser and the potential of this hillside.

The fourth basket strains under the weight of the biggest grapes

Fortunately, the next row over reassures you. You see a basket more than half full of plump, juicy grapes. You'd be proud to walk out of the vineyard with this basket. In Jesus' illustration, this branch bears *"more fruit"* (v. 2).

Can the harvest get better than this? Yes! Just wait until you feast your eyes on the basket in the last row.

Here, you immediately notice that both the size and the amount of the grapes are extraordinary. The fourth basket overflows with the biggest, most desirable grapes you've ever seen. You didn't know that one branch could produce so much. Jesus' description for this branch is that it "bears *much fruit*" (v. 5).

By the time you get home, you have a fuller sense of what Jesus was trying to say in the vineyard:

—Each of us is a branch that is producing a clearly defined level of abundance (which I have represented with baskets):

- Basket 1—"no fruit"
- Basket 2—"fruit"
- Basket 3—"more fruit"
- Basket 4—"much fruit"

—The Father wants more fruit from us so much that He actively tends our lives so we will keep moving up—from a barren to a productive branch, from an empty to an overflowing basket.

And more is always possible. Why? Because we were created to bear fruit, more fruit...and *still* more fruit!

Let me ask you, how much fruit do you see in your life today?

CREATED FOR ABUNDANCE

I've asked audiences all over the world how they would describe the level of fruit bearing among Christians today. Their responses are consistent. They conclude that nearly half of all Christians bear little or no fruit. Another third bear some fruit. Only about 5 percent bear a lot.

You'll see why some good-hearted Christians get stuck for years in turmoil, pain, and want.

Looking at the Christians you go to church with, do these numbers surprise you? Where do you fit in? If this portrait of God's people is even remotely true, you can immediately grasp the importance of the teachings from the vineyard. Bearing fruit is not some unique phenomenon reserved for certain kinds of Christians. It is the destiny of every believer.

If Jesus chose us for abundance, expects abundance, and created us to deeply desire it, how can we ever find fulfillment in a half-empty basket?

The answer is this: We can't, and we don't have to.

In the next six chapters you'll encounter three life-changing secrets from the vineyard. Each is a little-known or often-misunderstood principle that will unlock for you a life overflowing with fruitfulness for God. I don't call them secrets in the sense that they are known only to me, but rather that they are the key to solving a problem. Yet I can say with certainty that if you don't know *and* apply Jesus' vineyard teachings, you'll never experience the abundant life you long for. There is simply no other way.

If you suspect that your branch shows little or no fruit, the next two chapters are especially for you. We're going to look at that first empty basket and the barren branch that goes with it. You'll see why some good-hearted Christians get stuck for years in turmoil, pain, and want, and you'll understand why it doesn't have to be so. I guarantee that once you realize what God's invisible hand is doing in your life—and you then respond positively—you'll begin to flourish right away. And you'll wonder why you settled for so little for so long.

3

THE BEST
GOOD NEWS

(YOU DIDN'T WANT TO HEAR)

At a recent retreat I met a woman who seemed caught in an invisible net. Catherine was bright and articulate, a sixtysomething professional. When our dinner group shared about spiritual experiences, Catherine admitted that she had never been able to break through to a rewarding Christian life. "I just don't feel like my faith amounts to anything—except guilt. I always feel like God is unhappy with me," she said. "And why not? I don't make much difference for Him in the world."

Several times during the evening, Catherine wondered aloud why her faith wasn't working. About the time dessert was served, I had an idea. "I think there's something else that is keeping you spiritually stuck," I said.

"Like what?" she asked.

After we'd ruled out a few possibilities, I offered a

suggestion. "Could it be unforgivingness?"

"Why would you think that?" She seemed perplexed.

"Maybe I'm mistaken," I replied. But I offered to talk with her more if she wanted.

The next morning she was waiting for me after breakfast. She admitted to a long night with little sleep. Could I help her? We hadn't been talking long before bitterness toward her mother began spilling out. I asked her to list on a sheet of paper all the injuries and accusations she associated with her mother. The next morning Catherine met me again, this time trembling and clutching a sheaf of papers. She'd been crying.

"This is it," she said quietly. "This controls my life." She handed me five sheets, each covered on both sides in tiny script. Entry after entry laid out a bitter indictment against her mother. It added up to a lifelong chronicle of personal loss.

We talked. She wept. But by the end of the hour she was able to repent of her unforgiving spirit and release her mother. I saw her face soften as if the clock had turned back twenty years.

"Now you are ready to receive something new from God," I told her. And Catherine agreed.

Six months later I received a note from her. She told me she'd reconciled with her mother, but that was just the beginning. "I'm back on speaking terms with God," she wrote. "It feels like my soul is breathing again. Even my non-Christian friends have noticed. And I've started enjoying serving Him, too."

Like Catherine, millions of sincere Christians are caught in an invisible net. They experience pain. They feel like failures. Their lives show little or nothing of eternal significance, and they don't know why.

Are you one? If so, you are the believer Jesus was thinking about *first* that night in the vineyard. In this chapter we're going to look at barren branches and empty baskets. We'll ask how God responds to and treats a branch like

You are the believer Jesus was thinking about first that night in the vineyard.

Catherine's—one that bears nothing for an extended period of time. You'll face some hard realities that might alarm you. But you'll come to understand the priceless secret that can turn barren into beautiful.

If that's what you want, lean close…

THE BARREN BRANCH

Jesus said, "Every branch in Me that does not bear fruit He takes away" (John 15:2).

What a troubling thought! Some good Bible teachers have interpreted this verse to mean that if you bear no fruit, you can't be a Christian. Others have said "takes away" means if you persist in a life without showing evidence of your salvation, you lose it.

Something is stopping you dead in your spiritual tracks.

But don't you think the phrase "every branch *in Me*" should prove the main point here? The New Testament repeatedly describes the believer as "in Christ" (for example, 1 Corinthians 1:30; 2 Corinthians 5:17; Ephesians 2:10; and Philippians 3:9). Therefore, I believe we can safely conclude that it's possible to be "in Christ," yet be like that branch that produces no fruit for a time. Experience bears this out. If you're like me, you've gone a week or a year living in such a way that you know you didn't bear fruit. I believe that's what Jesus is talking about.

Besides, we know that salvation was never a work on our

part to begin with: "For by grace you have been saved through faith, and that not of yourselves; it is the gift of God, *not of works,* lest anyone should boast" (Ephesians 2:8–9).

And then there's Jesus' puzzling remark in John 15:3—"You are already clean." How is "takes away" related to "cleanness"? And what could "cleanness" have to do with "no fruit"?

The answer comes in two parts.

First, a clearer translation of the Greek word *airo,* rendered in John 15 as "take away," would be "take up" or "lift up." We find accurate renderings of *airo,* for example, when the disciples "took up" twelve baskets of food after the feeding of the five thousand (Matthew 14:20), when Simon was forced to "bear" Christ's cross (Matthew 27:32), and when John the Baptist called Jesus the Lamb of God who "takes away" the sin of the world (John 1:29).

In fact, in both the Bible and in Greek literature, *airo* never means "cut off." Therefore, when some Bibles render the word as "takes away" or "cut off" in John 15, it is an unfortunate interpretation rather than a clear translation.

"Lifts up" suggest an image of a vinedresser leaning over to lift up a branch. But why?

The second part of the answer came for me years ago at

a pastors' conference on the West Coast. A sun-browned man came up to me and asked, "Do you understand John 15?"

"Not completely," I answered. "Why?"

"I own a large vineyard in northern California," he said, "and I think I have it figured out." I offered to buy him coffee on the spot.

Lifting Up

As we sat across the restaurant table from each other, he began to talk about the life of a grower—the long hours spent walking the vineyards, tending the grapes, watching the fruit develop, waiting for the perfect day to begin harvest.

"New branches have a natural tendency to trail down and grow along the ground," he explained. "But they don't bear fruit down there. When branches grow along the ground, the leaves get coated in dust. When it rains, they get muddy and mildewed. The branch becomes sick and useless."

"What do you do?" I asked. "Cut it off and throw it away?"

"Oh, no!" he exclaimed. "The branch is much too valuable for that. We go through the vineyard with a bucket of water looking for those branches. We lift them up and wash them off." He demonstrated for me with dark, callused hands. "Then we wrap them around the trellis or tie them up. Pretty soon they're thriving."

As he talked, I could picture Jesus' own hand motions when He taught in the vineyard that night. He was showing how the Father makes sure His crop comes in full and sweet. When the branches fall into the dirt, God doesn't throw them away or abandon them. He lifts them up, cleans them off, and helps them flourish again.

Suddenly I had a burst of insight. *Lift up...clean....* I have never read John 15 in the same way again.

For the Christian, sin is like dirt covering the grape leaves. Air and light can't get in. The branch languishes, and no fruit develops. How does our Vinedresser lift us from mud and misery? How does He move our branch from barren to beautiful so we can start filling up our basket?

The answer to this question is the first secret of the vine.

FIRST SECRET OF THE VINE:

If your life consistently bears no fruit,
God will intervene to discipline you.

If necessary, He will use painful measures to bring you to repentance. His purpose is to cleanse you and free you of sin so that you can live a more abundant life for His glory.

The Bible calls this process discipline or chastening. I call it the best good news you didn't want to hear.

THE GOOD HURT

Discipline is what happens when our loving Father steps in to lift us away from our own destructive and unfruitful pursuits. "As a man disciplines his son, so the LORD your God disciplines you" (Deuteronomy 8:5, NIV).

I could picture Jesus' hand motions as He taught in the vineyard.

Of course, all of us are fallen creatures. We sin from time to time. But normally, God's discipline starts because of a major sin problem—an unconfronted behavior or attitude that is blighting your life. It ends when the problem ends.

Does discipline feel good to the child? No. (Maybe that's why we spend so much time trying to avoid it or to believe it doesn't happen.) Does disciplining feel good to the father? No. (If you're a parent, you know how reluctant you are to bring pain to your child. That's how God feels.)

Is discipline the way of committed love? Absolutely!

A key text for our understanding of how God seeks to clean us up is found in Hebrews:

> *"My son, do not despise the chastening of the LORD,*
> *Nor be discouraged when you are rebuked by Him;*
> *For whom the LORD loves He chastens,*
> *And scourges every son whom He receives."* (12:5–6)

We learn important principles from these verses:

- God is the source of the discipline,
- He disciplines all believers, and
- He always acts out of love.

Please notice that I'm linking "lift up"—the intervention of the Vinedresser in John 15—to the word *discipline* as it's used in Hebrews and elsewhere. *Airo* is not used elsewhere as a synonym for correction, only in Jesus' illustration of the vineyard. To make the connection, I have asked the broader question, *What does God do to wayward believers?* Answer: He takes necessary measures to correct them just as the vinedresser takes necessary measures to correct a wayward branch.

Why would a loving God want to bring us pain, even a small dose? To get our attention and to gain a highly desirable result from our life. As Hebrews 12:11 explains, "No chastening seems to be joyful for the present, but painful; nevertheless, afterward it yields the peaceable fruit of righteousness."

A parent knows how it works. You've repeatedly told Tyrone, your fearless five-year-old, that he's not allowed to cross the street. You're acting out of loving concern. But when Tyrone's favorite ball rolls into the street, he ignores the rule.

So you step in. Since your words haven't registered, maybe it's time to make him sit in the corner and repeat "I'm not allowed to cross the street" fifty times. Maybe you should confine him to his room for a spell. Or take away his prize ball. Tyrone balks, he resists, he wails...but you can't *not* act. Even if he can't fully appreciate the danger of moving vehicles, he can learn to associate that mistake with negative consequences.

Let's admit that many people misread God's discipline because of harmful personal experiences in their own childhood. You may be one. I encourage you to let the truth about your heavenly Father change how you think. This Father will never discipline you out of rage or selfish desire. He will never lose control. "Our fathers disciplined us for a little while as they thought best," says the writer of Hebrews, "but God disciplines us for our good" (12:10, NIV).

God's actions are all intended to nudge you—lovingly, wisely, persistently—toward the life and character you desire but can't reach without help.

It's All up to You

Once believers understand God's motive in discipline, an astonishing truth dawns: *The discipline doesn't have to continue! It's all up to me. I will only experience pain as long as I hang on to my sin.*

After all, the Vinedresser has only abundance and joy—not misery—in mind when He tends to a dirty branch. As soon as the branch is cleaned up and ready to thrive, the need for intervention ends. That's why my goal is to help you identify how God is dealing with you so you can avoid needless and extended discipline.

God doesn't expect you to seek out or enjoy His correction. If you're being disciplined, He wants you to get out of it even more than you want to.

And remember that His discipline is always just one aspect of His relationship with you. When your mother reprimanded you, she didn't stop caring for you, talking to you, or wanting your love in return. Satan would love to convince you that because your Father is dealing firmly with you, you're a worthless, unlikable loser. The opposite is true. Only if you've never received discipline should you doubt His favor. The Bible says, "If you are without chastening, of which all have become partakers, then you are illegitimate and not sons" (Hebrews 12:8).

HARD REALITIES

Is your branch sick? The first time most Christians recognize themselves in Jesus' teaching about discipline, they react with shock and sadness. Shock, because they failed for so long to connect troubling circumstances with God's purposeful intervention because of sin; sadness, because of all the unnecessary pain and turmoil they've endured, sometimes for years.

Catherine, the bright woman you met earlier, was trapped in a gray world of disappointment and pain. Yet she mistook these symptoms for the underlying problem—which in her case was unforgivingness, bitterness, anger, hatred, and vengefulness. Because of her sin, God was disciplining her. He wanted her heart and soul healthy and her life yielding fruit. Besides, He knew that deep down her empty basket was part of her misery.

Do you remember I said that the hard realities about God's discipline might alarm you? In the next chapter, you'll see how Christians can suffer from fatigue, illness, and even death because of long-term, unheeded disciplining. *Has God's discipline ever gotten that severe?* you ask. The answer will surprise you. It will also strongly motivate you to spend not a minute longer than necessary in the dirt and dust.

He knew that deep down her empty basket was part of her misery.

I've introduced you to part of the first secret: God always disciplines those who bear no fruit. But understanding how He goes about this—and how to respond to Him so that His correction can end—is the part of the secret that can take you to the next level of fruitfulness. That's where you get to trade in your empty basket for clusters of luscious grapes.

4

LOVE BY
DEGREES

onsider the power of a mother's eyebrow. When I
was a boy, my mother could snap me straight to
attention, jerk my still-empty hand from the
cookie jar, and clamp my mouth shut midchatter—all
with a single twitch!

I grew up in a family of six children. If one of us misbehaved at dinner, Mother's raised eyebrow was the first hint of trouble to come. That look meant, *Bruce, what do you think you're doing?*

What power her little warning had to end all sorts of foolishness! (I'm sitting up straighter now just thinking about it.) The truth is, my mother's eyebrow wielded great influence because I knew from experience what would happen next if I *didn't* pay attention.

I want to show you how the Vinedresser redirects His

children in a similar way. When we let sin block our ability to bear fruit, God intervenes. At first, with the gentlest gesture.

But what happens if you ignore Him? What if you assume that a "raised eyebrow" is as far as His discipline goes?

As you're about to find out, He lovingly raises the stakes.

In the last chapter we discovered that disciplining is God's proactive answer to moving you out of barrenness and toward fruitfulness. We identified sin as the cause of having little or nothing to show of eternal value in your life. Disciplining is the Vinedresser's strategy for cleansing you so you can start to produce fruit for your basket.

If you're still wondering whether you are in a season of discipline, ask yourself this question:

Can I look back over my walk with God and see very clearly that a sinful behavior I used to be caught up in is no longer an issue? Are there thoughts, attitudes, or habits that used to dominate my life but don't anymore?

If you can answer yes, you're moving forward and upward with God. If you can't, your basket is probably empty and you are undoubtedly being disciplined. I recommend that you now try to understand what degree of discipline God might be using to get your attention.

THREE DEGREES OF INTERVENTION

Do you have a clear sense of how God communicates His wishes for you when you need His correction? If we look again at the verses from Hebrews 12, we find three degrees of intervention. You'll never again need to live in confusion about how God is acting on your life to bring you back to fruitfulness.

The first degree of discipline can be as simple as a convicting thought, as arresting as hearing your name.

Degree 1: Rebuke—"*My son, do not...be discouraged when you are rebuked by Him*" (v. 5).
A rebuke is a verbal warning. If I was smart enough to respond to my mother's eyebrow at dinner, peace was restored. The family meal would unfold pleasantly for everyone. On the other hand, if I persisted in misbehavior, my parents would escalate their efforts. My father would clear his throat. That meant *Bruce, is it possible you didn't notice your mother's eyebrow?*

If I still didn't come to my senses, Dad would say my name—calmly, deliberately, and bristling with admonition: "Bruce!"

He wasn't picking on me unfairly. As the first degree of discipline, these rebukes were a result of my poor choices and were meant to spare me further pain.

We hear God's rebuke, even though we don't always choose to respond. God can make Himself heard in many ways: a prick of our conscience, a timely word from another person, a Scripture, the preaching of God's Word, or conviction by the Holy Spirit. (Do you see how wonderful and kind it is of God to use so many methods to get our attention and steer us away from peril?)

These verbal cues—like the frequent pleas of a mother with young children—are by far the most common kind of discipline we experience in God's family. We should always have our ears open for them. If, however, we harden our heart and close our ears, we force our Father to intensify the correction.

Degree 2: Chasten— "*For whom the* LORD *loves He chastens*" (v. 5). In other places in the Bible, the word *chastening* is used interchangeably with discipline. But in our text we find a specific use that shows a more serious degree of discipline.

Chastening is something you feel as emotional anxiety, frustration, or distress. What used to bring you joy now doesn't. Pressures increase at work, at home, in your health or finances.

For young Bruce at the dinner table, chastening might have meant being sent to his room until the meal was over. No more food. No more enjoying the company of family. The rebukes hadn't worked. Hopefully, an unpleasant feeling would.

Many Christians bump along in this level of discipline, yet fail to read the signs. They feel unfulfilled at church, critical of their Christian friends, and "on the outs" with God. When they pick up their Bible, it feels like a lead weight instead of a welcome relief. Their relationship with the Lord, like Catherine's in the previous chapter, seems blighted by a sadness or lethargy they can't quite trace.

If any of these symptoms sound familiar, you don't need to go to church more or try to read your Bible with a better attitude. You need to look for ongoing sin in your life, the dirt crusting over your leaves and cutting you off from God's best.

If you don't respond, love will compel your Father to take more drastic measures.

Degree 3: Scourge—*"And scourges every son whom He receives"* (v. 6). To scourge is to whip, to inflict punishment. It's the same word the Gospels use to describe what the Romans did to Jesus just before they crucified Him. Not a pretty picture!

In fact, for the word *scourge* you could substitute *cause excruciating pain*.

What percentage of Christians do you think have experienced scourging? It may shock you to read that God scourges "every son." That means you have most likely already been scourged in your life.

At this level of discipline you are living in open sin with a flagrant disregard for what you know is right. You have not heeded previous attempts by God to rescue you from rebellion and return you to fruitfulness. Therefore, He must resort to intense pain to bring you to your senses.

Consider wayward young Bruce. If nothing else worked to encourage decent behavior, my father would banish me to my room to wait for a spanking. My knees would rattle; my mouth would turn to chalk. I knew what was next—a paddling I'd never forget!

Pain—everyone hates it, but it sure does get your attention, doesn't it? C. S. Lewis said that God whispers through pleasure but shouts through pain. Sometimes our Father has to shout.

He takes long-term sin very seriously, and He will act. The consequences are more drastic than most Christians understand. Paul said that unconfessed and unrepented sin in the Corinthian church had cast an alarming pall over that little community. Members were living openly in grievous sins, yet sharing at the Lord's Table as if nothing were wrong. Paul said that their acts brought judgment to themselves and others. "That is why many of you are weak and sick and some have even died," he wrote (I Corinthians 11:30, NLT).

Did you get that? Because of continuing sin among believers, many were weak, many more were ill, and some had already died! This isn't an Old Testament incident; it happened in a New Testament church much like yours or mine.

Since so many Christians in our churches acknowledge that they are producing no fruit for God (which we have learned is a result of enduring sin), could it be that many among us are suffering dire consequences as a result?

What would you say to the evidence?

I'm keenly aware that this is challenging territory and we should proceed with several cautions:

- God would never hurt an innocent person to indirectly discipline a sinning person. In other words, your mother won't get cancer because you're living in an affair. (Would you send your son to his room because your daughter broke the rules?)

- When God does discipline us, it is never out of meanness, impatience, or wrath.
- God offers each of us opportunities to respond to Him, right up to the moment we leave this earth.

With these cautions in mind, we must still take Paul's warnings very seriously. I urge you to do so because, "The fear of the Lord is the beginning of wisdom" (Proverb 9:10). If the personal cost of long-term, serious sin can become so great, you have to wonder, *What keeps so many Christians from dealing with it and moving on into fruitfulness?*

I believe a leading reason is that they have let themselves become prisoners of damaging misconceptions.

WHAT STOPS GOOD PEOPLE FROM CLEANING UP THEIR ACT?

Beliefs are hard to spot. For one thing, to decide what we believe, we tend to listen to what we say instead of watching what we do. For another, we want the convenience our wrong beliefs afford so much that we convince ourselves that we must be right. I've met thousands of Christians who have been held captive by damaging beliefs for years.

Do you recognize yourself in any of these misguided voices?

- "The pain and negative circumstances in my life are the results of natural consequences or fate. They're not connected to my choices."
- "If God does discipline me somehow, it would probably be a one-time deal. He's much too forgiving to impose escalating consequences or to intentionally cause me pain just to motivate me to stop sinning."
- "Let's be honest. The enjoyment I get from my so-called sin outweighs any spiritual benefit I'd get from stopping. And anyway, my sins aren't really hurting anybody."
- "I simply can't help myself. This problem goes back to my childhood. So why wouldn't God extend grace rather than impose discipline?"
- "Just because I sin doesn't mean I can't do something for God. Hey, God uses crooked sticks. We can't all be Billy Graham, you know."
- "It's not a sin. It's just a weakness, part of my personality, something I struggle with."

If you recognize yourself in any of these misconceptions, do you see what you're really saying? *My sin doesn't have consequences. God won't pursue this. I like my sin too much to quit. I've convinced myself that I can't quit. My sin won't diminish my effectiveness.* And finally, *My problem isn't even a sin.*

If this is you, I encourage you to embrace truth, discarding the lies that have kept you stuck in unnecessary pain. Face the fact that the longer you stay in discipline, the more you are asking God to turn up the intensity of His corrective actions. Turn wholeheartedly away from the sin that has kept you from thriving and your basket empty.

One day you will wonder how you could have resisted your Father's kindness for so long and at such cost.

THE JOYFUL TURNING

The Bible word for this unforgettable, hope-filled change of direction is *repentance*. Repentance is a turning away from the sin that ails you to the bounty God promises you. One day you will look back on your former determination to stay in the dirt and wonder how you resisted your Father's kindness for so long and at such cost.

Responding to God's discipline brings immediate benefits. When we allow discipline to train us, we not only escape
our sin, but we also grow in maturity. Hebrews talks about
the "peaceable fruit of righteousness to those who have been
trained by it" (12:11). Repentance doesn't just get us back to
zero—God takes us from a minus ten to a plus ten.

Neither is repentance a one-time act. It is a lifestyle, an
ongoing commitment to keep putting aside our rebellion
and receive God's forgiveness. Some sins leave us in such
bondage that we need ongoing help and accountability. No
one knows this truth better than those who have overcome
serious addictions and brokenness in their pasts.

Yet each of us is invited to give God permission every
day to shape and cleanse and redirect us. With each turning
we enter more directly into an experience of God's pleasure.

In the next chapter you'll discover the secret of moving
from "fruit" to "more fruit." Every vinedresser knows that
once a barren branch starts to thrive, it holds great promise
for an abundant harvest ahead.

5

A COUNTRY
AWAKENING

One early spring Darlene and I moved with our family to the country. We needed to slow down. We were looking forward to enjoying the beauty of our new place.

A couple of days after we unpacked, I was puttering in my garage when I noticed my neighbor hacking down a row of grapevines that rambled along a fence on our shared property line. I had assumed that we owned the vines jointly. Wasn't that how things worked in the country? We already had visions of feasting on bucketfuls of grapes in the fall.

I walked over to say hi. My neighbor, a large, white-haired man in overalls, wielded the biggest set of shears I'd ever seen. All around him lay heaps of grape branches.

"You don't like grapes, I guess?" I said, trying to conceal my distress.

"Love grapes," he said.

"Really. Well, I thought maybe we would be sharing the crop from this vine and I..." I hesitated. Maybe it was too late to do any good.

He eyed my shiny shoes. "You're a city boy, aren't ya?" he said.

"Not exactly, but I—"

"Don't know about grapes, do ya?" he broke in, and went back to hacking at the vine.

I told him I knew I liked the taste of them. And I told him I had particularly liked the promising look of this row of grapes when I bought the place.

"You like big, juicy grapes?" he asked over his shoulder.

"Of course! My family does, too," I said.

"Well, son," he said, "we can either grow ourselves a lot of beautiful leaves filling up this whole fence line. Or we can have the biggest, juiciest, sweetest grapes you and your

"You like big, juicy grapes?" he asked over his shoulder.

family have ever seen." He looked at me. "We just can't have both."

IS THIS LOVE OR SHEAR MADNESS?

We've seen how God intervenes in our lives when our branch is bare because of sin. But what does He do when the branch of our life looks pretty good—like that gorgeous vine rambling down my fence line—yet our basket still has plenty of room left for more harvest?

In this chapter and the next, I'm going to help you understand the second secret of the vineyard. After Jesus told His disciples how the Vinedresser cares for the barren branch, He reached for a branch that showed rampant growth but produced only a few clusters of grapes. Listen again to what He said:

> *Every branch that bears fruit He prunes, that it may bear more fruit.* (John 15:2)

God's strategy for coaxing a greater harvest out of His branches is not the one you and I would prefer. His plan is to prune, which means to thin, to reduce, to cut off.

As unthinkable as it sounds—as contradictory as it

is—the Vinedresser's secret for more is...less.

Are you ready for a troubling truth that, once grasped, will free you to view the trials you're now facing in a new light? Even change how you feel about them and reward you with a beautiful harvest for God?

Then you're ready for the second secret of the vine.

SECOND SECRET OF THE VINE:

If your life bears some fruit,
God will intervene to prune you.

If necessary, He will risk your misunderstanding of His methods and motives. His purpose is for you to cut away immature commitments and lesser priorities to make room for even greater abundance for His glory.

PICTURES OF PLENTY

Looking at the branch in Jesus' hand that night, the disciples knew exactly what He meant by pruning. Vineyards had been a symbol of God's generous provision for Israel for almost two thousand years. The disciples knew grapes like an Englishman today knows tea. They understood that to get more from a grapevine, you have to go against the plant's natural tendency.

Recently, I read a gardening report that explained why:

> Because of the grape's tendency to grow so vigorously, a lot of wood must be cut away each year. Grapevines can become so dense that the sun cannot reach into the area where fruit should form.

Left to itself, a grape plant will always favor new growth over more grapes. The result? From a distance, luxurious growth, an impressive achievement. Up close, an underwhelming harvest.

That's why the vinedresser cuts away unnecessary shoots, no matter

The disciples knew grapes like an Englishman knows tea.

how vigorous, because a vineyard's only purpose is...grapes. In fact, pruning is a grower's single most important technique for ensuring a plentiful harvest.

For the Christian, rampant growth represents all those preoccupations and priorities in our lives that, while not wrong, are keeping us from more significant ministry for God. Without pruning, growing Christians will only be able to live up to a fraction of their potential.

The principle of pruning invites a revealing question about your spiritual life: Are you praying for God's superabundant blessings and pleading that He will make you more like His Son?

If your answer is yes, then you are asking for the shears. Pruning is how God answers your prayers that your life will please Him more and have a greater impact for eternity.

Pruning is how God answers your prayers that your life will please Him more and have a greater impact for eternity.

PROFILES IN PRUNING

In the vineyard, an expert pruner applies his skills in four specific ways: to remove growth that is dead or dying; to make sure sunlight can get to all fruit-bearing branches; to increase the size and quality of the fruit; and to encourage new fruit to develop.

Our Father the Vinedresser is guided by similar principles. To make room for the kind of abundance He created us for, He must first cut away parts of our lives that drain precious time and energy from what's truly important. His plan for pruning is anything but random, and He works in every life uniquely—what He judges as wasteful for me might be necessary to you.

In teaching this passage over the years, I have asked many "branch mates" to describe what pruning has looked like in their lives. Here are some of the things I've heard:

- Kyle, airline employee—"After I became a Christian, I noticed that my monthly night out with my old crowd from high school began to leave me feeling empty and out of place. So I quit going. Interestingly enough, a few months later I led one of the guys to the Lord."

  Through Kyle's dissatisfaction, God was showing him that an old activity was *dead or dying*. It took up time and energy, giving little in return. When Kyle let go of it, new results quickly showed in its place.

- LaShauna, mother of four—"God has been nudging me to let go of some selfish habits that have been hindering my marriage for a long time. Just accepting the challenge to change felt like pruning to me. But since I've been meeting weekly with an older woman in our church, I'm experiencing new freedom. I'm very thankful. So is my husband!"

LaShauna's self-oriented behaviors were choking out her ability to bear fruit in her marriage. God wanted *more sun to reach* her key relationship.

- Jared, college senior—"I had to decide which was more important—the perfect two-hour workout or dedicating more time to our growing campus ministry."

  God was inviting Jared to set aside more time to *increase the size and quality of the fruit* in his life.

- Howard, retired programmer—"I thought I would spend my retirement playing golf and traveling, but God has been showing me some golden opportunities in short-term mission service. I think it's time to do something new for God, something really outside my comfort zone."

  God is looking for *new fruit* from Howard.

If disciplining is about sin, pruning is about self. In pruning, God asks you to let go of things that keep you from His kingdom purposes and your ultimate good.

Pruning is how God changes the picture of your life from a basket that is almost empty to a basket that's starting to fill.

MISUNDERSTANDING GOD'S METHODS

Let's be honest—pruning is cutting and cutting hurts.

Sounds a lot like being disciplined, doesn't it? No wonder most Christians have trouble distinguishing between discipline and pruning in their lives. It all feels the same. But it isn't.

Jesus wanted His disciples to be very clear about the difference. Why? *Because the purposes of discipline and pruning are entirely different, and because the consequences of confusing them can be disastrous!* Jesus knew that if His future followers misread the Vinedresser's actions in their lives, they would come to the wrong conclusions about the Vinedresser's purpose and plan.

If disciplining is about sin, pruning is about self.

I know. For years I struggled with anger and confusion because I mistook the process of pruning for discipline. When intense periods of distress seemed to lay siege to me, my family, or my ministry, I turned things upside down looking for the kind of major sin that would warrant the discomfort I was experiencing. I asked Darlene to help me see what I was missing. I pleaded, "What else do you *want* from me, Lord?" I confessed every known sin and waited for relief. But when nothing changed, I frequently slipped into anger toward God, then into bitterness, then mistrust. The result was a break in my relationship with Him.

And here's the distressing irony: Over time, those wrong reactions to pruning became a four-lane freeway that took me out of pruning and right back into God's discipline.

What a vicious and unnecessary cycle! I see now that if I hadn't finally grasped the difference, I could have been at odds with God for the rest of my life. But listen—vast numbers of Christians I talk to are stuck in the same misunderstanding, repeating the same detours, and getting the same painful results. In fact, I now believe that misreading God's actions or motives in pruning is the number one reason mature Christians unnecessarily slide back into discipline.

Does this scenario describe your life? Does it explain some spiritual detours in your past? Thankfully, the secrets of the vine can help you put this problem to rest forever. You won't need to spend another day fighting against God and losing when you can be working with Him to win.

PRUNING VERSUS DISCIPLINE—WHICH IS IT?

You can distinguish pruning from discipline by asking a few simple questions. I encourage you to carefully review the accompanying chart. If you suspect that you are being pruned, follow these steps:

1. Acknowledge that God is trying to get your attention. Decide that you don't want this season of turmoil to go to waste.

2. Trust that since a loving parent would tell a child why he or she is receiving correction, your loving Father will do no less. Believe that He wants you to know whether you are experiencing discipline or pruning.

3. Ask the Lord to help you answer this question: *Do I have a major sin that's causing You to discipline me?*

4. Pray, *Lord, I want to know. If You do not show me within a week from today that it is discipline, then I will take it by faith that it is pruning.* From my own experience, I can assure you that God has many ways to let you know if sin

Issue	Disciplining	Pruning
How do you know it's happening?	Pain	Pain
Why is it happening?	You're doing something wrong	You're doing something right
What is your level of fruitfulness?	No fruit (represented by Basket 1)	Fruit (represented by Basket 2)
What is the Vinedresser's desire?	Fruit (represented by Basket 2)	More Fruit (represented by Basket 3)
What needs to go?	Sin	Self
How should you feel?	Guilty, sad	Relief, trust
What is the right response?	Repentance (stop your sinning)	Release (give God your permission)
When does it stop?	When we stop sinning	When God is finished

is the issue—you will find the truth in a Scripture, a conversation, a teaching, or a phone call from a friend.

5. If you conclude that you're being disciplined, sin is the problem. Repent and turn around. You'll never regret it.

6. If you conclude that you're being pruned, your response is just as crucial, and the rewards will be even greater. Ask God to show you clearly what He wants you to let go of, and trust Him enough to release it completely to Him.

Is There Something You Should Say to God?

Imagine a sunny day in Indiana. Darren, twenty-five, has driven up from Memphis to see his dad, whom he's hardly spoken to for years. They're out in the driveway shooting a few hoops. Finally Darren gets out what he has driven so far to say:

"Dad, I didn't understand you for years. I didn't know why you had so many rules for me in high school—about parties, TV, chores, driving, money. I didn't like your expectations. I thought you were mean and stupid. I said terrible things about you behind your back. And, Dad, I'll admit that I hated you at times. But now I see that you were just trying to be a good dad. You only wanted what was best for me. You never gave up or gave in.

"I came here to apologize for what I have thought and said about you. I was wrong. I know I hurt you very deeply, and I'm sorry."

I believe that the majority of believers need just such a conversation with their Father. I remember the day I finally made amends with God over how I had been treating Him. That was many years ago, and I can tell you that it has radically improved my relationship with God.

Isn't it amazing that God allows Himself to be hurt by us? (We know this happens because Ephesians 4:30 says, "Do not grieve the Holy Spirit.") It's hard to comprehend God's tender love in the face of our misunderstanding, repeated rejection, and unwarranted abuse from us. Yet His love remains constant!

If your relationship with your Father is injured, I encourage you to apologize today for your attitudes and thoughts. Tell God you have misunderstood His actions and badly misjudged His character. Tell Him exactly how you have felt and why, and ask Him for His forgiveness.

GIVING GOD PERMISSION

Darlene and I don't live in that house with the grape arbor anymore, but I've thought about my country awakening many times since. I can still see that row of grapevines in September, its branches thick with clusters of purple fruit. I can still see the kitchen table groaning under boxes and baskets of grapes. I can taste the sweetness. I can smell the vats of jams and jellies bubbling on the stove. I can see our daughter stirring the pot and juice running down our boy's chin.

Abundance is such a beautiful thing, isn't it!

You might be looking down the fence line of your life right now, seeing branches being hacked off, feeling assaulted by circumstances—maybe even by God Himself—and wondering what God will do next.

I must tell you that your heavenly Father loves you so much that He won't stop tending your life. As you'll see in the next chapter, accepting the pruning process doesn't mean that your life, or your enjoyment of it, will shrink. The most fruitful *and* the most joy-filled Christians are the most pruned Christians!

6

FLOURISHING
UNDER THE SHEARS

Did you know that growers prune their vineyards more intensively as the vines age? One horticultural bulletin I read explained why:

> The vine's ability to produce growth increases each year, but without intensive pruning the plant weakens and its crop diminishes. Mature branches must be pruned hard to achieve maximum yields.

If you look at the future from a maturing plant's point of view, there's considerable cutting in store. But from the grower's point of view, the future holds something wonderful—grapes, grapes, and *more* grapes!

In this second chapter on pruning, I want to show you what God is doing to take you to that fuller basket of fruit in your life. While early pruning is mostly about your outward activities and priorities, mature pruning is about your values and personal identity. God moves in close for more intensive pruning because by now you are ready to really produce.

What God asks of you now may seem difficult. But the results, if you say yes to the Vinedresser, will be dramatically more than you could have imagined.

Many Christians never get this far. In fact, if you're not really committed to reaching the next level of abundance—*more* fruit—you probably shouldn't read this chapter. When Jesus told His friends what it would cost to follow Him, many turned back. Yet the impact of those who didn't is still shaking the world. If you know by now that God has a unique and important destiny for you—and you want it with all your heart—this chapter will take you across the next threshold to your future.

THE TESTING OF YOUR FAITH

I find it helpful to think of mature pruning in terms of the Bible phrase, "the testing of your faith." By the time they wrote their epistles, the disciples had learned to see every trial as a chance to perfect their trust in the Lord and multiply their effectiveness for Him. "[Let] the testing of your faith...have its perfect work," wrote James, "that you may be perfect and complete, lacking nothing" (James 1:3–4).

In mature pruning, the pruning will intensify as God's shears cut closer to the core of who you are. God isn't trying to just *take away*; He's faithfully at work to *make room* to add strength, productivity, and spiritual power in your life. His goal is to bring you closer to the "perfect and complete" image of Christ.

God isn't trying

to just take away;

He's faithfully at work

to make room to add.

Tests of faith have nothing to do with the status of your salvation—that's a settled fact. Neither are these tests on the level of "Why doesn't God help me find my car keys?" Tests of faith are various trials and hardships that invite you to surrender something of great value to God *even when you have every right not to.* You will feel assaulted or stretched by circumstances, but not distant from God; tried by Him, but not judged or guilty. A psalmist described the refining experience...and the priceless result.

For you, O God, tested us;
You refined us like silver....
But you brought us to a place of abundance.
(Psalm 66:10, 12, NIV)

Have you ever realized that a "test of faith" doesn't really test anything unless it pushes you past your last test? Past what you've proven on a previous test? That's why pruning often lasts longer and goes further than we think is reasonable or fair. And that's also why if you pull back when you reach what seems like your limit, you will never grow or know how much you can *really* trust God.

When your faith feels pressed to the limit, remember some important pruning truths:

God doesn't apply pain when a more pleasant method would do just as well. Pruning is always the only and best answer to our deepest desires; it is the tender gift of an all-wise and all-loving Father. "Pain was the loving and legitimate violence necessary to produce my liberty," wrote Blaise Pascal.

Not every painful experience is the result of pruning. Is your heart breaking because your teenager is experimenting with drugs and sex? God did not cause your son to do these things in order to prune you. Are you suddenly facing a future with diabetes or prostate cancer? God isn't purposefully constraining your life just to see how you'll react. Yet every trial you face is an *opportunity* to let Him work in your life for abundance. If you invite Him into your circumstances, He will keep His promise to work everything together for your good (Romans 8:28).

The pain of pruning comes now, but the fruit comes later. Just as in the vineyard, pruning in our lives is seasonal. But the quantity and quality of the future harvest depends on our submission to the Vinedresser now.

A "test of faith" doesn't really test anything unless it pushes you past your last test.

Even though the duration, depth, and breadth of pruning seasons will vary, no season lasts indefinitely. A season is coming, I promise, when you will *know* that you are no longer under God's shears. Everywhere you look you'll see amazing evidence of personal transformation and expanded ministry for God.

Consider the many trials Paul endured. Then consider the incredible size of Paul's harvest. It's impossible even to measure, isn't it? Paul's branch is *still* yielding fruit today.

Which leads us to a very important question: If a

supernatural harvest is what you really want, how can you tell exactly where God is pruning you so that you can cooperate with Him?

"TELL ME WHERE IT HURTS"

Jesus' conversation in the vineyard proves that God never intended pruning to be a mystery or confusing to us.

When you were a child and you injured yourself, your mother's first question when she saw your tears was,

"You refined us like silver.... But you brought us to a place of abundance."

"Where does it hurt?" When God is pruning you, you hurt somewhere in particular. The pain comes from the point where His shears are snipping something away.

If you are confused about where God is pruning you, ask yourself the same question: Where does it hurt? Through pain, God gets your attention and signals His urgency. The discomfort says, "Pay attention here."

First Samuel 25 tells the memorable story of how God used the pain test in David's life to prepare him for a remarkable future. He had already been anointed as Israel's next king, yet for years God seemed to abandon him. The former giant killer and national hero was reduced to hiding in caves to try to escape the murderous hatred of King Saul. You can read his spiritual journals from this excruciating season in Psalms 54, 57, and 63.

One day, out of hope and near starvation, David instructs his men to politely ask a nearby estate owner named Nabal for food.

"Who is this David?" Nabal roars, and refuses the request. That humiliating rejection is a direct hit to David's sorest point—his pride, not to mention his confidence, his sense of fairness, and his identity. Enraged, David sets out with his fighting men to slaughter Nabal's entire household.

But Nabal's wife, Abigail, hears what has happened and rushes out to intercept David. She brings a caravan laden with supplies. But her most important gift is an impassioned reminder to David that his real identity and the security for his future are safe in God's hands. In effect, Abigail pleads with David to see beyond his pain and choose instead to pass his test of faith. David recognizes her wisdom and turns back.

That crisis—coupled with his terrible years in the desert—was part of the pruning season necessary to prepare David for his future as Israel's greatest king. He learned how to submit to authority, to lead men, to endure, and to trust God in trying circumstances.

Your mother's first question when she saw your tears was, "Where does it hurt?"

Where does it hurt in your life today? Look for the Vinedresser's shears at work—shaping, directing, and strengthening you for a season of abundance that you may not be able to see right now, but that is nevertheless on its way.

PRIME POINTS OF PRUNING

Mature pruning is God's way of helping you put into practice His command to "seek first the kingdom of God." This is why God will always prune those things that we slavishly seek first, love most, and begrudge giving up. Again, His goal isn't to plunder or harm, but to liberate us so that we can pursue our true desire—His kingdom.

This kind of pruning goes beyond rearranging priorities to the heart of what defines us—the people we love, the possessions we cling to, our deep sense of personal rights. These are the very arenas God must rule if we are to bear fruit.

Let me share some pruning stories from my own journey as a disciple. Each story shows a key arena where, sooner or later for every mature believer, God's shears *will* be at work:

Arena 1. The people you love most.

I'll never forget a war that raged on a pink shag rug in a little girl's bedroom in Iowa. I was in Des Moines for a seminar, staying with friends. They had put me up in their little girl's bedroom. Everything was pink and small, and my feet hung over the end of the bed. But as I lay in that little bed, I found myself praying for a larger life. "Lord," I prayed out loud, "we've come so far. What is next?"

"Your kids," He said. I told Him I loved my kids.

God said, "Give Me your kids."

I didn't have to think. "Nope," I said. "You can't have them."

Have you ever arrived suddenly at a pruning point like that? Surrender does not even seem to be an option. The hours ticked by. I found myself kneeling on that pink battlefield, wrestling with God. Not until 3 A.M. was I finally able to release my children and my wife into His keeping. When the transaction was done, those dearest humans in my life no longer belonged to me. I am still privileged to love and tend them, but ownership rights have passed over to God.

God may be asking you to give up your "right" to be married, to have children, or to achieve a particular kind of success. God may be inviting you to follow Christ without the support of your closest family members—possibly even enduring their hatred and rejection because of your faith. If so, He is pruning closely to what really matters to you—not to take something good from you, but to become Lord of all you desire.

Arena 2. Your right to know why God does what He does.
We're born with the conviction that we deserve to be in control of our lives. Yet this assumption is in conflict with the life of faith. That's why very early in mature pruning, God will ask you to give up your "right" to

know *why* certain things are happening to you.

When he was very young, I took our son David to the hospital for a shot. As the doctor approached with needle in hand, David bolted. When I finally cor-ralled him behind a planter and swung him up into my arms, I saw the terror in his face. How can you explain to a sick toddler that his body needs penicillin? Yet David stayed in my arms as the doctor prepared to give the injection. When the moment came, David didn't push me away. Instead, he held on more tightly and cried out, "Daddy!"

His goal isn't to plunder or harm, but to liberate us so that we can pursue our true desire.

We go through long seasons in our faith walk when we're unable to answer questions like Why? and How long? We only know Who—our loving Father—and He has proven worthy of our trust. He asks us to let go of rea-sons, of rights, of fears, and simply throw our arms around His neck. At those times we can pray: "Father, I'm hanging on to You. You can do whatever You want. Just carry me through."

Arena 3. Your love for money and possessions.

For most of us, shedding the power that possessions and material comforts hold over us is a lifelong process and one of the most difficult. I've found that the "love of money" springs up like a noxious weed.

I found myself kneeling on that pink battlefield, wrestling with God.

Servitude to money and possessions demands our energies, our time, and our loyalties. That's why, season after season, the Vinedresser asks us to let go of the things we still hold too tightly. Is God asking you to release something to Him, either literally or in your heart?

To know where you are in this process, ask yourself: How much of what's mine has God already asked for? And have I given it to Him?

If we allow this process of pruning to continue, an exuberant freedom to bless others will flourish in its place. This beautiful outcome is described by Paul in a letter to the Corinthians: "We want you to know about the grace that God has given the Macedonian churches. Out of the most severe trial, their overflowing joy and their extreme poverty welled up in rich generosity" (2 Corinthians 8:1–2, NIV).

Arena 4. The sources of your significance.

The prize at stake here is your God-given need for a sense of worth and purpose. For Abraham, it was his miracle son, Isaac. For Gideon, it was his large army. What is it for you?

For me, it was the ministry of Walk Thru the Bible. I struggled for years to give back to God what I understood to be my life's work. The final test came when I grew increasingly sure that God wanted me to make an executive decision that I knew could end the ministry.

I felt like God was asking me to give Him my life's dream. I vacillated. I postponed. Finally, the day came when I put the future of Walk Thru on the altar. I informed our team that we would no longer support the ministry in this way. When I got home, I told Darlene that this chapter of our life was over. To the forced-choice question of God or my ministry, I had chosen God.

But Walk Thru did not close its doors. Once I chose God, He blessed the ministry in ways I never imagined. I understand now that during that period of pruning, God was bringing me to a critical juncture in my Christian life. In order to reach the next level of abundance, I would have to completely give back to Him the work He Himself had given me, trusting only in Him for what would happen next.

GRAPE EXPECTATIONS

The apostle Paul wasn't in the vineyard that night with Jesus and the disciples, yet he became a veteran of pruning. He began, by his own description, as "of the people of Israel, of the tribe of Benjamin, a Hebrew of Hebrews...a Pharisee, as for zeal...as for legalistic righteousness, flawless" (Philippians 3:5–6). But by the end of this life, we glimpse a rare thing indeed: *a man who had been pruned until there was nothing left of his self-life.* All that made Paul who he was—his job, position, heritage, pride, religion—had been pruned away.

He asks us to let go of the reasons and throw our arms around His neck.

In his final letter from prison, he wrote, "But what things were gain to me, these I have counted loss for Christ. Yet indeed I also count all things loss for the excellence of the knowledge of Christ Jesus my Lord, for whom I have suffered the loss of all things, and count them as rubbish, that I may gain Christ" (Philippians 3:7–8).

By now, Paul didn't need to order his priorities. He

had only one. "But one thing I do," he wrote, "Forgetting what is behind and straining toward what is ahead, I press on toward the goal to win the prize for which God has called me heavenward in Christ Jesus" (vv. 13–14, NIV).

You may be thinking, *Sure, a spiritual giant like the apostle Paul can live a life of radical pruning, but is that really what God wants for me, too?* For your answer, don't miss Paul's closing exhortation: "All of us who are mature should take such a view of things" (v. 15, NIV).

Here is a testimony to the goal of mature pruning: that you will finally be so surrendered to God that everything you now love dearly—even worthy activities and goals—will be let go into God's sovereign keeping. What remains in your grip is one passion, one goal, one unhindered opportunity: *to bear more fruit.*

The truth is, Christians who have experienced deep pruning don't focus on what is left behind anyway. They're given to courageous, hope-filled, forward-straining prayers on the order of this one from author John Piper:

> *Lord, let me make a difference for you*
> *that is utterly disproportionate to who I am.*

YOUR RESPONSE IS EVERYTHING

In the last two chapters, we've been talking about how God acts in our lives to move us from "fruit" to "more fruit," from a basket with some fruit in it to one with a lot. My goal is to help you recognize what is already happening in your life so you can cooperate with God...and move to the next level of abundance.

If we let Him, an exuberant freedom to bless others will flourish.

I am not inviting you to ask for pruning. Trials *will* come. The question is simply whether or not you will let the purposeful pruning of God do its work in you, or let it go to waste.

In pruning, *how* you respond makes all the difference. You can complain, rebel, compromise, or run away. Or you can experience the joy, comfort, and rest that come to disciples who keep their eyes on the prize, not the pain. Listen to Peter describe how some Christians in his day were triumphing in the middle of severe testing:

In this you greatly rejoice, though now for a little while, if need be, you have been grieved by various trials, that the genuineness

of your faith, being much more precious than gold that perishes, though it is tested by fire, may be found to praise, honor, and glory at the revelation of Jesus Christ, whom having not seen you love. Though now you do not see Him, yet believing, you rejoice with joy inexpressible and full of glory.
(I Peter 1:6–8)

Here, at this point of believing with joy, the last secret of the vine opens to you. You are ready to experience the sweetest abundance of all: the mystery Jesus called abiding.

7

MORE OF GOD, MORE *WITH* GOD

I was driving to work one bright Georgia morning when a black Corvette pulled alongside me, top down, paint gleaming. The driver looked cool and confident in his designer sunglasses. Seconds later, the sports car roared past and disappeared over a rise.

That's when I noticed it—something was missing. Sure, I still had my wallet and the clothes on my back. I still had my job, complete with a long to-do list. I still had a wife and kids at home. But my heart was gone. It had been stolen and was now speeding away with that Corvette.

By the time I walked into my office, I was in a full-blown crisis—already contemplating resigning, maybe taking a job at a parking lot. The ministry that just yesterday had seemed so important, today tasted like sawdust.

I went home that night and talked things through with Darlene. We decided that the problem might be burnout. For months I'd been working harder and longer, but I seemed to have less to show for it. By bedtime we had come to the disturbing conclusion that the passion I used to feel about serving God had been in decline for some time. The black Corvette actually had little to do with my dilemma. All it had done was steal the illusion that everything was fine.

A black Corvette stole the illusion that everything was fine.

Instead of resigning, I started to pray. For days I pleaded with God to show me what to do. He seemed to nudge me toward calling a man I'd met more than ten years earlier. George is a respected leadership mentor and scholar on the West Coast. When I got on the phone, I struggled to put my problem into words.

"Bruce, are you having money troubles?" George asked. I said no. "Something to do with sex?" No, nothing like that.

By the time I hung up, he had invited me to fly out to California to see him.

"I Know Why You're Here."

A few days later, George and I were settling into two big red leather chairs. Outside the window, eucalyptus trees swayed in the breeze. "Tell me your whole life story," he said, "and don't hurry."

I talked for at least an hour. When my account came to two years before the present, George stopped me. "Let me finish your life story," he said.

"But how can you?" I asked. "You don't even know what has happened!"

"But I know why you're here," he said. He got up to pour me a fresh cup of coffee, then continued. "I've studied over five hundred Christian leaders' lives—biblical examples, historical figures, and contemporary people, some of whom you know. And, Bruce, you're right on schedule."

"On schedule for what?" I asked. George definitely had my attention.

Standing in front of me, he held up his hands, palms facing me. "These are your two sources of fulfillment. My right hand stands for your relationship with God, my left for your competence in ministry," he said. "When you first began to serve the Lord, your relationship was young and vibrant. It had to be because your competence was weak." He moved his right hand up so that it was higher than his left.

He continued. "But over time your competence increased." He moved both hands to a side-by-side position. "At this stage, the fulfillment you experienced from your competence approximately equaled the fulfillment you experienced from your relationship with the Lord."

George's left hand drifted upward, above his right hand. "Pretty soon, your competence became apparent to all. You had never been more productive for God. But your walk with Him began to suffer. Your satisfaction dropped." He paused. "Bruce, this is where you are now."

I was in the stage, he said, when most throw even more energy into their work, hoping to recapture their former fulfillment. But it doesn't work for long. Some drift into affairs, leave the ministry, retreat from their lifelong commitments. "Bruce," he said, "the Lord is saying, 'Put relationship with Me first'—that it's time to switch hands again. If you do, you'll find the joy that you're missing now, and so much more."

In less than two hours, George had cut to the core of my distress: my relationship with God. It was an eye-opening, yet difficult, moment for me.

Does any of my story ring true for you? Looking back now, I can put what George was telling me into vineyard terms:

You have a good amount of fruit. You are not being "lifted up" in discipline. And you are not being pruned. Yet you feel caught between two opposing tensions— an *increasing desire* to produce an even better yield and *decreasing fulfillment* in the fruit you are already producing.

George stopped me. "Let me finish your life story," he said.

You are ready for that fourth basket, the one so full of luscious grapes that it is overflowing. Yet you feel frustrated, defeated, and in danger of losing the harvest of a lifetime.

And you have no idea what to do.

By the time I got up from George's leather chair, a simple but intimidating truth had dawned on me: God didn't want me to do more *for* Him. He wanted me to be more *with* Him.

I was ready for the final secret of the vineyard.

YOUR PLACE TO REMAIN

After seeing God act in your life through chastening and pruning, you might think that you are now a candidate for the perfect program, perhaps a sophisticated New Testament strategy for multiplying growth in yourself and others. After all, if fruit equals good works, then surely "much fruit" must equal many more works.

In abiding,

it's always our move!

But in Jesus' final remarks in the vineyard, He turned the disciples' attention away from activity altogether. I imagine Jesus leaning forward in the circle of light that spring evening. I see Him tracing the gnarled curve of an ancient vine, His fingertips pausing where the massive trunk divides into a branch.

"Abide in Me, and I in you," He says.

Then He directs the disciples' attention down the branch—trimmed and tied along the trellis and already swelling with the promise of the harvest to come.

> *"As the branch cannot bear fruit of itself, unless it abides in the vine, neither can you, unless you abide in Me."*

Do His friends understand what He's saying? Are they even paying attention? His eyes sweep the circle.

"I am the vine, you are the branches. He who abides in Me, and I in him, bears much fruit; for without Me you can do nothing."

At this critical moment, Jesus tells what should happen next—after discipline to remove sin, after pruning to change priorities.

Abide in Me...

Picture the place where ancient trunk meets vigorous branch. Here is the touch point, the place where abiding happens. Here is the connection where life-giving nutrients in the sap flow through to the developing fruit. The only limitation on the amount of sap that goes to the fruit is the circumference of the branch where it meets the vine. That means that the branch with the largest, least-obstructed connection with the vine is abiding the most and will have the greatest potential for a huge crop.

This picture brings us to the final and most abundant category of fruitfulness, the third secret of the vine.

THIRD SECRET OF THE VINE:

*If your life bears a lot of fruit,
God will invite you to abide more deeply with Him.*

His purpose is not that you will do more for Him but that you will choose to be more with Him. Only by abiding can you enjoy the most rewarding friendship with God and experience the greatest abundance for His glory.

To abide means to remain, to stay closely connected, to settle in for the long term. With this picture Jesus is showing the disciples how an ongoing, vital connection with Him will directly determine the amount of His supernatural power at work in their lives.

Within six verses in John 15, Jesus says *abide* ten times. You can sense the passion and poignancy of His plea. Jesus knows that He is about to leave His friends, yet He is saying, "We must be together." He knows that in the coming years, these downcast, frightened men now standing with Him in the vineyard will be called to produce an unheard-of, miraculous amount of fruit—enough fruit to turn the whole world upside down.

And Jesus knows they can't begin to achieve that kind of eternal impact without the one thing they're most likely to forget: more of Him.

MYSTERIES OF ABIDING

"Abide," Jesus says. Don't miss the command. *Abide* is an imperative—not a suggestion or request. You don't have to command a child to eat dessert. You command someone to do something because it's not going to come naturally.

In the seasons of chastening and pruning, the Vinedresser is proactive. He pursues. He initiates. Our role is to respond. But with abiding, we see a 180-degree shift in who initiates the movement toward fruitfulness at the highest level. To abide, we must act.

So even though abiding is not about doing more, if we want to experience it, we must do *something*—and the effort won't come easily. In abiding, it's always our move!

Notice, however, that we are helpless to bear much fruit alone. "The branch cannot bear fruit of itself...for without Me you can do nothing" (vv. 4–5). Imagine a grape branch, severed from the trunk and lying in the dust. For that severed branch to produce one new leaf, flower, or grape would be impossible.

Jesus goes on to say, "If anyone does not abide in Me, he is cast out as a branch and is withered; and they gather them and throw them into the fire, and they are burned" (v. 6).

These words sound catastrophic, but Jesus isn't threatening a barren branch with hell. Unlike the olive tree, whose wood has found many uses since ancient times, the grape produces wood that is brittle and small. Ezekiel wrote, "Is wood taken from [the grapevine] to make any object?... Instead, it is thrown into the fire for fuel" (Ezekiel 15:3–4). Jesus is making a dramatic point. If we are not abiding, we wither and die and become of no spiritual use.

Finally, notice the implied promise for the branch that *does* abide. If you stay connected to Him, if you draw spiritual nourishment from Him, if you allow the power that flows through Him to flow through you, nothing will hold you back from reaching the most abundant life possible.

THE URGENCY OF NOW

"The next move is up to you," George told me that day as I prepared to leave for home. But he gave me a warning: Unless my friendship with God became my first priority, George predicted that I would never fulfill my true destiny as a Christian or a leader.

"You'll feel God tugging on you only for so long," he said. "Your crisis of unhappiness is very important. If you don't break through now, you might never do so."

The news was sobering. Here I was, feeling that my life's work no longer brought me fulfillment, *but I was not supposed to work directly on the problem.* Rather, I needed to put all that aside and focus on something else, something that came much harder for me, something that seemed infinitely more elusive.

You might be wondering why a Bible teacher and leader of a large Christian organization would

"You'll feel God pushing you only for so long," he said.

have let his relationship with Christ slip into second place. To be honest, I wondered the same thing. Make intimacy with God my *first* priority? I already prayed and read my Bible regularly. So what had gone wrong?

By the time I got back home from my visit with George, I was determined to find the answer.

8

LIVING IN
THE PRESENCE

When I arrived home from my meeting with George, I made three simple commitments to the Lord for the next year. I would:

- get up at 5 A.M. every day to read my Bible;
- write a full page in a daily spiritual journal;
- learn to pray and seek Him until I found Him.

I still remember the first line of my first spiritual journal: "Dear God, I don't know what to say to You."

Day after day I would look at what I had written. On every page I saw the real reason my busy Christian life now left such a bland taste in my mouth—I'd become an expert at serving God but somehow remained a novice at being His friend.

But I stayed with it. By the middle of the second month, things started to shift. It was as if a great Presence walked into my room in those early morning hours and sat down near me. My rambling journal entries gradually became personal confessions to the Listener. His passion for me, His purposes for my life—not just for the *idea* of my life, but for that particular day, hour, and minute— began to rise up from the pages of my Bible.

That was more than fifteen years ago. The pleasures of abiding—and the extraordinary benefits—have redefined the scope and impact of God's work through me. I see fruit everywhere I turn. Yet not even one grape is a result of working harder.

I assure you that I possess no special knowledge in these matters—generations of seasoned disciples have traveled ahead of me down this road. Yet, as far as I can tell, the great majority of God's people today live ignorant of the promise and practice of abiding. As a result, they fail to reach the level of "much fruit" represented by that fourth, overflowing basket.

Maybe you're among that majority. You're not sure how an overflowing spiritual experience actually happens. And you might be asking, "How could merely abiding possibly propel me to the highest levels of fruitfulness?" My prayer is that in the next few pages you'll find answers.

THE PERSON OF ABIDING

Abiding is all about the most important friendship of your life. Abiding doesn't measure how much you know about your faith or your Bible. In abiding, you seek, long for, thirst for, wait for, see, know, love, hear, and respond to...*a person.* More abiding means more of God in your life, more of Him in your activities, thoughts, and desires.

It was as if a great Presence walked into my room in those early morning hours and sat down near me.

In our Western-style rush to do and perform for God, we often falter at the task of simply enjoying His company. Yet we were created to be dissatisfied and incomplete with less. In the words of the psalmist, "As the deer pants for the water brooks, so pants my soul for You, O God" (Psalm 42:1).

If our need for this relationship is so deep and constant, why do so few of us fervently pursue it? One of the primary reasons, I'm convinced, is that *we don't really believe God likes us.* Sure, we believe God loves us in a theological sense ("God loves everybody, right?"), but we don't feel particularly *liked* by Him. We're convinced that He remembers all the bad things we've done in the past and is quick to judge how we're doing now. We assume He's impatient, busy with more important things, and reluctant to spend time with us.

Why would you want to spend time with a person who felt that way about you?

If you were to list the qualities of your best friend, I expect you would note things like "She accepts me," "He always makes time for me," and "I always leave her presence feeling encouraged." What you appreciate in a best friend is precisely what God offers. He is trustworthy and patient. When He looks at you, He does not call to mind the sins you've asked Him to forgive. He sees only a beloved child, a worthy heir.

And this God—your Friend—wants to abide with you even more than you want to abide with Him. Jesus said, "As the Father loved Me, I also have loved you; abide in My love" (John 15:9). Did you catch that? *Stay, luxuriate, find real love "in My love"*!

If we really abided in His love, we would come away

feeling so nourished, so cherished, so liked, that we would rush back to Him whenever we could.

THE PRINCIPLES OF ABIDING

When you start with the Person of abiding and realize how much He loves you and wants to share His life with you, you have taken the most important step toward the practice of abiding.

Think again about the meeting place of vine and branch. Why would Jesus give us a picture of a living thing whose life force—the sap—is mysteriously out of sight? One reason could be that in abiding, what happens on the surface doesn't count; what's happening inside does. Abiding begins with visible spiritual disci-

I'm convinced that we really don't believe God likes us.

plines, such as Bible reading and prayer. Yet it may shock you to find out that *we can do these things for years without abiding.* After all, reading a book about a person isn't the same thing as knowing the person who wrote the book. The challenge in abiding is always to break through from dutiful activities to a living, flourishing relationship with God.

Annie, a mother of four, wrote to tell me about her recent breakthrough:

> I'm not just reading my Bible or making requests anymore. I listen for Him, meditate on His Word. I write down what I hear Him saying to me. I try to make this time as honest, deep, and intimate as possible. When I started out doing devotional times, it was like I was getting my time card stamped by heaven—"Yep, she was here. A whole ten minutes!" Lately, I've had to drag myself away.

I see two principles that will help you discover the kind of experience Annie describes. Both have to do with how you spend your time.

Principle 1: To break through to abiding, I must deepen the quality of my devoted time with God.

Notice that I didn't say "devotional time." That might imply that the purpose of your time with God is to have devotions. I use the word *devoted* in the biblical sense of something set apart for God. In Psalm 27, David expresses his desire for this kind of time with God:

One thing I have desired of the LORD,
    That will I seek:
That I may dwell in the house of the LORD
    All the days of my life,
To behold the beauty of the LORD
    And to inquire in His temple. (v. 4)

All the how-tos that follow are intended to help you create and enjoy "set apart" times with the Person of God.

Set apart the kind of time that will build relationship.
Some Christians I know try to have their meaningful personal times with God just before bed, but I have yet to find a respected spiritual leader throughout history who had devotions at night. Unless you get up early, you're unlikely to break through to a deeper relationship with God. Set aside a significant time and a private place where you can read and write comfortably, think, study, talk to God out loud, and weep if you need to.

In abiding, what happens on the surface doesn't count; what's happening inside does.

Savor God's words to you.

When you read your Bible, receive and savor it like food, like a treasure, like a love letter from God to you. Remember, you're reading in order to meet Someone. Ponder what you have read, and apply it to your present circumstances. Let it go down into the core of your being. And as you read, expect Him to commune with you. Paul advised, "Let the word of Christ dwell in you richly" (Colossians 3:16).

Talk and listen to a Person.

So often, when we turn to prayer, we treat God like He's some mystical force "out there." But God wants you to talk to Him like you would a friend. He wants to hear your requests, your worries, and your praise and thanks. Risk being honest, and expect His insight in return. Take time to be still before Him. Decide to seek the Lord until you find Him.

Keep a daily written record of what God is doing in your life.

I recommend that you keep a spiritual journal—not a diary of your day, or an attempt at literature, but a living record of your very personal journey with God. Share with Him your disappointments, celebrations, and confusions. Ask Him for wisdom…and leave your request on the page until you receive guidance. Keep track of His answers. I believe that men in particular need a tool like journaling to bring a sense of reality to their relationship with our invisible God.

Unless you get up early, you're unlikely to break through to a deeper relationship with God.

Remember, these simple practices are called disciplines because they take effort. But the reward is worth it!

Principle 2: To break through to abiding I must broaden my devoted time—taking it from a morning appointment to an all-day attentiveness to His presence.

Too many of us leave God in the study or beside our favorite chair and go on with life. But the lessons of the vine show us that so *much more* is possible!

One day, in a library, I happened upon a lithograph of a legendary vineyard set on a rocky hillside high above

Germany's Rhine Valley. The illustration showed vines that had been producing bountiful harvests for generations. An inset depicted one of the vines. It came out of the ground thick as an elephant's trunk. All along the row, enormous clusters of grapes hung down through the light canopy of leaves.

For years people wondered how these vines could flourish in such an inhospitable environment. An accompanying text explained: "The roots of the ancient plants have been traced to the distant river."

That ancient vineyard reminds me that I can always be "present" with God, no matter what is whirling around me. God invites each of us to be tapped into His purposes and power *all the time*.

Brother Lawrence, a seventeenth-century lay Christian who worked in a monastery kitchen, described his practice of abiding in God: "I do nothing else but abide in His holy presence, and I do this by simple attentiveness and an habitual, loving turning of my eyes on Him. This I call...a wordless and secret conversation between the soul and God which no longer ends."

How could this work in a busy person's life? Annie shared her experience:

I'm putting away groceries, and the kids are tearing through the house with the bags over their heads, screaming. I can be a little frazzled, but inside I'm saying, "Jesus, You are here with me, in me, around me. Thank You for food and for my noisy kids." I'm not always successful at this, but I try to take Jesus with me wherever I go. We keep each other constant company.

OVERCOMING BARRIERS TO ABIDING

If abiding is the key to unlimited abundance, why are there so few Annies? I believe the answer goes beyond laziness or indifference. Many have never been taught what it means to abide. Others are hindered by damaging misconceptions, such as the idea that God doesn't really like them. Here are two more misconceptions that keep good people from the riches of abiding.

Misconception 1: Abiding is based on feelings.
Communion with God is a relationship, not a sensation. That will come as a huge relief if you think you must have an emotional rush or sentimental feeling when you spend time with God. You won't always, and you don't need to.

We understand this in our marriages and other significant friendships. My love for Darlene is constant—but my feelings for her are far different during an argument than they are during a candlelight dinner. We don't measure the depth of our relationship by our feelings at any particular moment.

Communion with God is a relationship, not a sensation.

Abiding is an act of faith—a radical expression that you value God's unrestricted presence in your life more than any immediate sensation. If you think you must always have strong feelings in order to know you've been with God, you'll go away from your devoted times disappointed. Before long you'll say, "Abiding just didn't work for me."

Misconception 2: We can abide in Jesus without obeying Him.
Jesus told His friends in the vineyard, "If you keep My commandments, you will abide in My love" (John 15:10). We might paraphrase what Jesus is saying like this: "If you want to abide with Me, you have to go where I'm going. When you go your own way, you're on your own."

Disobeying always creates a breach in your relationship with God. You can enjoy an emotional worship experience on Sunday but if you pursue a sinful lifestyle during the week, you will never succeed at abiding.

MORE FOR LESS

If you're at all like me, by now you're struggling with the basic math of abiding. It may sound a bit fishy, like one of those fast-food TV ads promising more beef for less bucks. You're wondering how working less *for* Him in order to spend more time *with* Him can add up to "much fruit" in your life.

One reason is that when you abide, God rewards you by supernaturally multiplying your efforts. I've experienced this firsthand more times than I can count. But there are other reasons why the third secret of the vineyard—*abiding more, doing less*—leads us to more results for God. These have to do with the benefits of abiding—what happens to us and through us when we consistently practice it.

Abiding helps us to sense the leading of the Lord. We learn to recognize God's "still small voice" (I Kings 19:12) and become familiar with His ways. Abiding helps us to accomplish more for Him because we are more in tune with His directives.

Abiding helps us to tap into all of God's spiritual riches. As we saw with the illustration of the vineyard in Germany, when we're abiding, we can draw deeply from God's resources. The disciples learned this principle, and it was evident as they healed and preached. In Acts 4:13 we read, "Now when they saw the boldness of Peter and John, and perceived that they were uneducated and untrained men, they marveled. And they realized that they had been with Jesus." When we abide, we are "with Jesus" and are filled with His Spirit and power.

By the miracle of His life in us and with us, we will realize our greatest achievements.

Abiding gives us the "rest" we need to bear a much greater yield. When we spend intimate time with our Savior, we are strengthened and refreshed to do His work.

Abiding carries with it a promise of answered prayer. Jesus said, "If you abide in Me, and My words abide in you, you will ask what you desire, and it shall be done for you. By this My Father is glorified, that you bear much fruit" (John 15:7–8). Later, in verse 16, Jesus repeats the promise, and again it is directly connected to the disciples' mission of bearing fruit.

Nothing pleases God more than when we ask for what He wants to give. When we spend time with Him and allow His priorities, passions, and purposes to motivate us, we will ask for the things that are closest to His heart.

ONE FOR THE RECORD BOOKS

By the miracle of God's life in you and with you, you will see fruit of such quantity and size in your life that you will be amazed, and *you will know that you had nothing to do with it.*

Undoubtedly the most startling symbol of abundance in the Old Testament is this snapshot of what the spies found in the Promised Land: "They came to the Valley of Eschol, and there cut down a branch with *one cluster of grapes; they carried it between two of them on a pole*" (Numbers 13:23, emphasis added). Have you ever heard of such an astounding harvest?

My friend, keep that snapshot of supernatural abundance in your mind because it is the portrait of fruitfulness that God has in store for you!

9

JOYFUL
ABUNDANCE

The scene for our story shifts from the vineyard at night to Galilee one early morning several weeks later. Waves murmur on a stony beach and mist hangs over the surface of the lake.

Not far offshore, Peter and several other disciples are working their nets when they hear a voice calling from the beach.

"Friends, do you have any fish?"

The fishermen call back, "No!" It's been a long, fishless night.

The voice comes back—"Cast the net on the right side of the boat, and you will find some!"

You know this story from John 21 well, don't you? You know that, apparently without hesitation, the men in their battered boats pull in their nets and fling them over the other side. Soon they haul up such a net-straining catch of fish that they know beyond doubt who that man in the mist is.

"It is the Lord," John says to Peter.

And you know what Peter does next. In your mind's eye, you can see Peter look toward shore. You can see him drop his hold on the net, plant his foot on the bow of the boat, and take that beautiful, flying leap into the waters of grace.

Every word of this book is intended to help you take that leap. When Peter jumped, he forever left behind his little dreams of success. He left behind his doubts about God's plans for him and his stubborn insistence that things should turn out according to his expectations. He left behind any thought that his sins outweighed God's forgiveness.

That impulsive leap marked the moment of Peter's breakthrough to a life of remarkable abundance. We read about it in the book of Acts, where God used him to be the new church's first leader, to preach to thousands, and to bring healing and the Holy Spirit. And we see it again in his earnest letters, so full of a passion he called "joy inexpressible and full of glory" (I Peter 1:8).

Are you standing precariously at a launching point in your life? Do you hear a voice calling? It is the Lord.

I hope you jump.

LITTLE MAN, HUGE HARVEST

If you've read the first book in this BreakThrough Series, you have met another person who took his own extraordinary leap. His name was Jabez. Instead of launching from the side of a boat, Jabez (whose name means "pain") kneeled in the dust of an ordinary life and prayed a daring prayer for abundance. In I Chronicles we read:

> *And Jabez called on the God of Israel saying, "Oh, that you would bless me indeed, and enlarge my territory, that Your hand would be with me, and that You would keep me from evil, that I may not cause pain." So God granted him what he requested.* (4:10)

Of the more than five hundred names recorded there, only the name of Jabez receives this kind of special comment. Why? I believe his little prayer distills into a few words what it means to leap wholeheartedly into the life of fruitfulness God wants for His children.

Jabez's epitaph could read:

Here lies Jabez
Born in pain,
died with honor,
because he dared
to ask of God
what God most wanted to give.

I can report that more than three thousand years later, God is answering Jabez's prayer in remarkable ways! Around the world today, millions of Christians are taking the Jabez challenge because they want to bear more fruit in their lives for His glory. Like Jabez, these believers are praying every day for God's blessing, for more influence for Him, for His hand of power to be upon them, and for His protection from evil.

Don't miss the link between the Jabez prayer and the secrets of the vine: Your Jabez prayer invites God to use you to bear fruit; the secrets of the vine reveal how God changes you so that you will become even more useful (fruitful) for His glory.

The message of *Secrets of the Vine*, like *The Prayer of Jabez* before it, is grounded in a simple but profound assertion: that we unlock change in our lives and in our world when we choose to do God's will in God's way...and it all begins with asking.

YOUR FATHER'S FACE

There's a memorable moment in John Steinbeck's American classic *The Grapes of Wrath*. As a dust storm approaches, an Oklahoma farm family has gathered in front of their house to watch. The working men in the family are looking toward the horizon, silently pondering their chances of escaping disaster. The children hang onto their parents' knees and watch the horizon, too. But the women watch only the men's faces. All that really matters to the women, they can find written there.

Have you seen your Father's face lately? I can't think of anything else that would tell you more about your present state or your future prospects. Allow me to paint a picture of what I see:

If you are in the season of discipline, the Vinedresser is kneeling beside you in the cool of the morning. He is reaching down to intervene in your life, to lift you up and bring you back to fruitfulness. The look on His face conveys concern and sadness—not disgust, not irritation, not even anger. He doesn't see a chronic loser in you, but a chosen, carefully tended branch that is one choice away from an altogether better existence.

If you are in the season of pruning, the Vinedresser is standing beside you in the sun of midday. He's wielding some rather serious-looking shears, but He's not unhappy. In fact, the look on His face conveys delight and expectation. As He thoughtfully snips away unwanted shoots, He's impressed with your energy and promise. He can foresee the time when you will respond in faith to the test He has put before you today.

If you are in a season of abiding, I see the Vinedresser leaning against a nearby trellis as the sun is going down, his hat pushed back. He's looking at your branch with pleasure, satisfaction, and joy. Just being here near you, enjoying your beauty, is His favorite moment of the day. The huge clusters of grapes crowding your branch are exactly what He's had in mind for you since your branch first sprouted.

Now that you know how God is always at work in your life, and you see His face of love toward you, you need never again misunderstand His ways.

BEWARE THE GRAPE ROBBER

Of course, misunderstanding and suspicion are exactly what your enemy wants. Through his devices of doubt, distrust, discouragement, and deception, Satan tries at every turn to prevent or steal your harvest and keep you from reaching greater fruitfulness.

To guard the harvest of good works for God in your life, consider these important reminders:

God can use you no matter what season you're in. In fact, while we are predominantly in one season at a time, the seasons do overlap. The enemy wants to discourage and confuse you. He will tell you that until you're at the next level, God certainly won't choose to use you in any meaningful way. But God can and will use you, whatever season you're in. Jesus used His disciples to preach the kingdom and even perform miracles while they were still immature in their faith.

God's plans for you are unique and specially suited for your success. Each branch requires individual attention because the Vinedresser knows our individual needs and the pattern of our responses. Don't compare your progress to anything or anyone but God's gracious will for you.

It's never too late to begin bearing fruit. The grape robber tries to convince Christians that we've missed our chance to respond to the Vinedresser. Yet while God wants each of us to respond now, He'll continue to pursue us our entire lives.

You can rest in God's sovereign timing. If you're primarily being disciplined or pruned now, the enemy may try to discourage you about your small yields. Stand firm in knowing that God has already prepared a significant life for you that He will faithfully bring into being (Philippians 1:6).

Remember the gift of joy. Your enemy will point to the pain of discipline, the losses that came with pruning, and the frustration and effort associated with abiding, and he'll try to convince you that God's plan for you is a prescription for misery. But remember Jesus' wonderful promise to His disciples that night in the vineyard: "These things I have spoken to you, that My joy may remain in you, and that your joy may be full" (John 15:11). As the disciples proved in the years to come, that promise of full joy is a reality you can build a life on.

A DISCIPLE'S DEEPEST DESIRE

I've always been so glad that Peter swam *toward* the Lord he had so recently denied. The silhouette of that fisherman diving from the boat is an unforgettable picture of every disciple's lifelong desire for God.

During Peter's long swim to shore, if not before, I think he remembered his first encounter with Jesus (told in Luke 5). On that occasion, too, Jesus had told Peter and his fishing partners where to put down their nets for a catch. Then, too, they had caught so many fish that their nets had started to sink. After the men had hauled the harvest ashore, Jesus had told Peter, "From now on you will catch men" (v. 10).

Maybe by the time Peter was close enough to shore to see his Lord's face, he had finally put it all together....

Catch men.

Bear fruit.

You see, many days after His "final words" in the vineyard, Jesus was still having the same conversation—still trying to show His followers the same big picture of abundance, this time using the symbol of fish instead of grapes:

Do you have abundance? You were created for a life-mission of abundance for God. But you can't accomplish the work of your Father's kingdom on your own.

Do you want more abundance? More is always possible, but you'll have to do something opposite of what you're currently doing. You'll have to cooperate with God's ways and respond in obedience and trust.

No matter what season of fruit bearing you are in, when you look at your Father's face, I hope you see what Peter saw when he clambered, dripping and hopeful, out of the lake that morning.

He saw a breakfast of mercies waiting and a future as big as God's love.

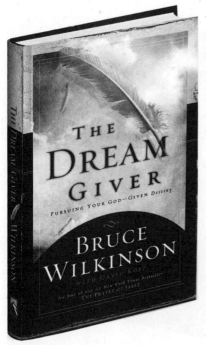

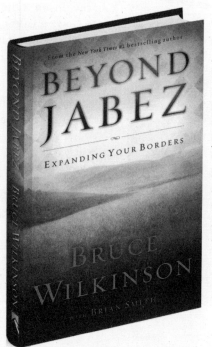